BOOK ANALYSIS

Written by Emmanuelle Laurent

Trans

Dom Juan

BY MOLIÈRE

Bright
≡Summaries.com

Shed new light
on your favorite books with

Bright
≡Summaries.com

www.brightsummaries.com

MOLIÈRE   1

French playwright, actor and stage manager

DOM JUAN   2

Dom Juan or the punished libertine

SUMMARY   3

CHARACTER STUDY   9

Dom Juan
Sganarelle
Elvira

ANALYSIS   13

The master and the valet
The master's complexity and the valet's simplicity
Dom Juan - another Tartuffe?
Hypocrisy, a privileged vice
The arrest of the impostor and the divine punishment of the libertine
Characteristics of the Baroque
Dom Juan, a Baroque character?
The Myth of Don Juan
Molière's Dom Juan
Evolution of the character

FURTHER REFLECTION   25

Some questions to think about...

FURTHER READING 27

MOLIÈRE

FRENCH PLAYWRIGHT, ACTOR AND STAGE MANAGER

- **Born in Paris in 1622**
- **Died there in 1673**
- **Notable works:**
  - *Dom Juan* (1665), comedy
  - *The Miser* (1668), comedy
  - *The Bourgeois Gentleman* (1670), comédie-ballet

An author, director, stage manager and actor, Molière (whose real name was Jean-Baptiste Poquelin) was born in Paris in 1622 into the affluent bourgeoisie. Very early on he decided to pursue a career in the theater and founded, along with actress Madeleine Béjart, the Illustre Théâtre company. After twelve years of travelling theater in the provinces, he returned to Paris where he was noticed by Louis XIV who took him into his service.

He wrote mainly comedies in which, under the cover of humor, he highlighted the defects of his contemporaries (preciosity, pedantry, avarice, etc.) and criticized 17th century society (authoritarian fathers, religious hypocrisy, quack doctors, etc.). His many plays are still influential today, making Molière one of the most important authors of the classical century.

He died in Paris in 1673.

DOM JUAN

DOM JUAN OR THE PUNISHED LIBERTINE

- **Genre:** theatre (comedy)
- **Reference edition:** Molière (2006) *Dom Juan*. Paris: Éditions Larousse.
- **First edition:** 1665
- **Themes:** seduction, debauchery, hypocrisy, religion, baroque

Dom Juan was performed for the first time in 1665. The play was a huge success for its first fifteen performances, until Molière was accused of impiety and of having deliberately chosen Sganarelle – Dom Juan's opponent – as a poor defender of religion.

Borrowed from the Spanish comedy and Italian theatre, this tragicomedy mixes genres and does not respect the rule of the three unities. The play was never published during the author's lifetime, but was rediscovered in the centuries that followed, and the "great Lord become an evil man" that Molière condemned became a fascinating myth.

SUMMARY

ACT I

Scene 1

Gusman, Dona Elvira's horseman, comes to ask Sganarelle, a valet, the reason for their master Dom Juan's precipitated departure, when he has just taken the young woman from her convent in order to marry her. Sganarelle answers that "a marriage costs him nothing to contract" and "a great lord become an evil man is a terrible thing".

Scene 2

Dom Juan arrives and Sganarelle warns him of Dona Elvira's presence. Dom Juan tells him that "another object has chased Elvira from [my] thoughts" and justifies his inconsistency: according to him, "all the pleasure of love subsists in change".

Scene 3

To Elvira, who immediately realizes that Dom Juan doesn't love her anymore, he offers a religious scruple as explanation: "I believed that our marriage was but adultery in disguise." The religious hypocrite makes his first apparition in Dom Juan's character, which provokes Elvira's anger.

ACT II

Scene 1

Pierrot, a peasant, tells Charlotte, a peasant girl, how he saved a master and his valet from drowning. He describes the gentleman's lavish costume. Then, he reminds Charlotte that they are to be married.

Scene 2

The master and his valet mentioned by Pierrot are none others than Dom Juan and Sganarelle. Dom Juan failed in his attempts to seduce the young woman he had in mind, but this object of desire is quickly replaced by another: a peasant girl, Charlotte, who seduces him and to whom he offers marriage.

Scene 3

Pierrot enters the stage and expresses his jealousy. Instead of making excuses, the great lord slaps the peasant.

Scene 4

Mathurine arrives, a woman to whom Dom Juan promised marriage first. Dom Juan plays a double game, promising marriage first to the one, then to the other, in private discussions. Sganarelle warns the peasant girls: "My master is a scoundrel [...] he is the groom of the entire human race".

Scene 5

His swordsman warns Dom Juan that twelve men on

horseback are looking for him. Dom Juan asks Sganarelle to switch clothes with him to allow him to escape his pursuers.

ACT III

Scene 1

In order to not be killed instead of Dom Juan, Sganarelle suggests another disguise to his master: Dom Juan in country clothes, Sganarelle as a doctor. Sganarelle interrogates his master about his beliefs. Cautious, Dom Juan only answers: "I believe that two and two makes four, Sganarelle, and that four and four makes eight."

Scene 2

Lost in the woods, the two men ask for directions from a beggar who lives on charity. Dom Juan offers him a gold piece, provided that he swears against God. The beggar refuses.

Scene 3

Upon seeing a man attacked by three others, Dom Juan, in the name of his aristocratic ideal, comes to his aid. It is Carlos, Elvira's brother, who came looking for Dom Juan to make him pay for the insult to his sister.

Scene 4

Dom Alonse, Elvira's other brother, arrives and recognizes Dom Juan. He wants to kill him, but Dom Carlos prevents him from doing so in the name of the same code of honor, as Dom Juan just saved his life: he suggests they postpone their revenge.

Scene 5

Dom Juan and Sganarelle come across a mausoleum and the statue of the commander, who Dom Juan just killed. Out of foolhardiness, he invites the commander to dinner. The statue answers positively by lowering its head.

ACT IV

Scene 1

Sganarelle does not doubt that "Heaven, [...] has produced this miracle" to convince his master to repent.

Scene 2

Mr. Dimanche, one of Dom Juan's creditors, is announced.

Scene 3

Thanks to his pleasantries, Dom Juan manages to send his creditor away with no more payment than a few words.

Scene 4

Then Dom Louis, Dom Juan's father, tired of his son's behavior, reminds him of what is due to his aristocratic origins, and that "birth is nothing without virtue". Dom Juan answers with a final insolent remark.

Scene 5

Sganarelle, who condemns the son's attitude towards his father, is forced to remain silent out of fear.

Scene 6

Elvira arrives, covered in the veil of the convent to which she retired. Heaven left in her heart "only a flame purged of all the commerce of the senses": she tries to save Dom Juan from a final impenitence that would seal his damnation.

Scene 7

While Elvira has "reawaken[ed] in [him] a few embers of a doused fire", Dom Juan dines in the company of his valet. Someone knocks on the door. It is the statue of the commander.

Scene 8

The statue sits at the table and invites Dom Juan to dinner for the following day.

ACT V

Scene 1

Dom Juan announces to his father his sudden conversion: "the sudden change that Heaven has made in me will surprise all the world".

Scene 2

However, Dom Juan is actually still the same and he admits to his valet that this sudden change was only "a useful stratagem" to sweet-talk his father and secure his affairs. Hypocrisy, "a privileged vice", has wonderful advantages: "it is the true way to do with impunity all that one wants".

Scene 3

To Dom Carlos, who has come one last time to demand that Dom Juan take on the wife he abandoned, the latter answers that his conversion makes it impossible and that he "took counsel with Heaven about it".

Scene 4

Sganarelle is indignant: "Sir, what style are you taking now?"

Scene 5

The ghost of a veiled woman appears and invites Dom Juan to repent. But the libertine refuses Heaven's mercy and shows every sign of strengthened sinning.

Scene 6

The statue of the commander appears: Dom Juan feels an invisible fire consuming him, a chasm opens, and the earth swallows him up. Sganarelle concludes: "Look at that, everyone satisfied with his death! [...] No one is miserable but me [...] My pay! My pay! My pay!"

CHARACTER STUDY

DOM JUAN

Dom Juan, who dominates everything with his overwhelming presence, ends up defeated after all. In this complex character, Molière exposes surprising contrasts. He is represented as a man of "quality", belonging to a great family and showcasing some of the traits linked to his origins: elegance, courtesy, natural seduction, artful language, knightly courage. Yet everything lowly he does contrasts with his very high nobility.

His successive facets – the libertine lover (Act I), the atheist (Act III), the hypocrite (Act V) – are the result of a logical progression: libertinism in matters of the heart leads to libertinism in matters of the soul, which leads to false devotion. As Dom Juan does not believe in love, he does not believe in God, and as the libertine seduces women, the hypocrite abuses men. Molière managed a crescendo, making his character less and less appealing to the audience, and making hypocrisy the worst vice and the sin that will lead to his eternal damnation, as explained by Sganarelle: "All you lacked before to perfect your arsenal was this hypocrisy!" (Act V Scene 2). Because he has defied God, it is God Himself who punishes him, after having offered him His mercy, which he refuses. The spectacular death of Dom Juan, with thunder and lightning and the black chasm of hell, is like the character, both flamboyant and dark, a living contradiction, a baroque oxymoron (figure of speech linking together two contradictory words).

SGANARELLE

There is no theater couple more united than Sganarelle and Dom Juan, who are always together in nearly all the scenes. The valet is tied to his master by necessity ("My pay! My pay! My pay!") and by fear: "With me, fear performs the office of zeal". As the play mixes up genres, he is simultaneously the traditional comic valet, cowardly, talkative, fond of good food, and a tragic confident, as when Dom Juan, hypocritically, shows him the bottom of his soul.

He is his master's accomplice, a sort of inferior double who even acts like him out of complacency and mimicry. When his master is far, he becomes his judge. As cowardly as his master is brave ("What? Scoundrel, you run when they attack me?" Act III, Scene 5), he can only oppose his master's rigorous logic with a stupefied silence or a disorderly discourse: "What a man! What a man!" (Act V Scene 2). Although he tries to prove God's existence with the classical argument of the final causes (man's perfection commands a creator), when he interrogates his master about his beliefs, he mentions the Bogey-Man, a figure of popular superstitions. This is why those who accused the play of impiety reproached Molière for having chosen Sganarelle as a defender of religion.

However, Molière has other defenders of religion scattered throughout the play:

- The beggar: confronted with Dom Juan, who has become the face of temptation to make him commit a mortal sin

by swearing, he refuses: "I would rather die of hunger" (Act III Scene 2)
- Dom Louis, Molière's representative, who reminds him that "birth without virtue is nothing" (At IV Scene 4)
- Donna Elvira

ELVIRA

This character is creation of Molière. Dom Juan has seduced this religious sister of noble birth to get her out of convent and marry her, thus already positioning himself as God's rival.

Elvira appears a first time as an injured wife who demands justice. Her true and unique love contrasts with Dom Juan's multiple conquests, who is incapable of loving and to whom she has to lend the words which she would have liked to hear: "Why not swear that your sentiments for me are unflinching, that you've always loved me with the same unparalleled ardor, and that nothing can part you from me except death?"

This true love grows even purer and becomes "a holy tenderness". Touched by grace, she appears veiled in Act IV, wearing the habit of the convent to which she returns: "You see me quite changed from what I was this morning". This scene is the exact counterpart to the scene where Dom Juan also pretends that he has been touched by divine grace, before admitting that he hasn't changed. Elvira's agape (spiritual love) is opposed to Dom Juan's Eros (physical love), "a detached love, which does not act at all for itself"; she comes to save Dom Juan from a final sin that would lead him to damnation. But unable to be moved by the language of the heart, he is sensitive only to the eroticism of Elvira. She will appear one last time in the form of a veiled ghost, the embodiment of mercy, which Dom Juan refuses.

ANALYSIS

THE MASTER AND THE VALET

An inseparable couple

Dom Juan, present in 25 scenes out of 27, is always followed by Sganarelle, present in 26 scenes. There is a constant subordination of the one to the other, to the point where the valet sometimes appears as the inferior double of his master.

Sganarelle, Dom Juan's accomplice

Fearing a beating, Sganarelle is forced to "applaud[ing] what [his] soul detests" (Act I Scene 1). Confronted by Elvira who demands an explanation, Dom Juan asks his valet to answer for him: "Madame, here is Sganarelle, who knows why I left" (Act I Scene 3). To escape his pursuers, the master suggests to his valet that they switch clothes: "Happy is the valet who can gain the glory of dying for his master" (Act II Scene 5). Like his master, Sganarelle encourages the beggar to commit blasphemy ("Go ahead, swear a little, there's no harm" (Act III Scene 2); like him, he sends away the creditor, Mr. Dimanche, in order not to pay his debts.

Sganarelle, Dom Juan's judge

Reduced to silence when in the presence of his master, the valet "pours his heart" when he is far (Act I Scene 1), or when he speaks quietly. The audience is therefore painted, thanks to these asides, a blackened portrait of Dom Juan:

"Ah! What an abominable master I am obliged to serve!" (Act I Scene 3). As he lives in close contact with his master, Sganarelle believes he knows him well: "I know my Dom Juan like the back of my hand" (Act I Scene 2). However, Dom Juan escapes his grasp, just as he escapes ours. The valet can, at the most, sketch some of his characteristics: "Yet this is only a sketch of the character, and to finish the portrait I would need a lot of paint" (Act I Scene 1). Dom Juan's portrait therefore remains unfinished.

THE MASTER'S COMPLEXITY AND THE VALET'S SIMPLICITY

Psychological depth

As he is mainly meant to provoke laughter, Sganarelle remains restricted by the traditional traits of the comedy valet. His master has a psychological depth which he lacks. Faced with his valet's common morale, Dom Juan proclaims the freedom and aristocratic audacity of being oneself, challenging both God and society.

The great lord

The qualities - and faults - of Dom Juan result from his perception of his own worth, which places him above the laws, but also from his manners, his knightly courage and the elegance of his discourse. It is mainly through his language, his weapon for seducing women, that his superiority is shown. Through an implacable argumentation, he destroys the logic of false devotion, while Sganarelle, who tries to demonstrate God's existence or to condemn his master's hypocrisy, can only oppose incoherent exclamations: "Heavens! Am I hearing this?"(Act V Scene 2).

The play's meaning

Which side does Molière support? The play's critics reproached him for having chosen in Sganarelle a poor defender of religion. This claim is true, just as he is cowardly and superstitious. Does this mean that Molière sides with Dom Juan, secretly approving his libertine behavior? It is hard to confirm, because although the libertine and atheist have a certain charm, the religious hypocrite is irksome; similarly, the 'gentleman' who, through his wrongdoings, ignores the rules of civility, is for the 17th century man an "abomination to nature".

Molière, as always, sides with the characters who represent measure and honesty: Elvira, the beggar, Dom Carlos and Dom Louis, defend that which Dom Juan opposes better than Sganarelle could ever do. However, it is the valet who announces from the start the tragic fate awaiting his master.

DOM JUAN - ANOTHER TARTUFFE?

Tartuffe's struggle and Dom Juan's struggle

When *Dom Juan* was first performed on stage, on 15th February 1665, *Tartuffe* was still forbidden. One year later, as Molière was under surveillance, he stopped the play's production after fifteen performances, despite the public acclaim. Act V of *Dom Juan* is Molière's answer to his adversaries, to whom he shows a religious hypocrite who unveils his imposture, but who will later be unremittingly condemned.

The great lord and the peasant

While Dom Juan is a religious hypocrite "out of pure policy", Tartuffe is a "peasant" without resources, a professional impostor: he is the figure of the parasite. Sensual, "round and red, bursting with health and excellently fed" (Act I Scene 4), he doesn't have Dom Juan's elegance, who, though religious hypocrite, remains nonetheless a great lord. For the latter, the mask of the hypocrite is yet another way to express his sovereign freedom, "to play its game in peace with a sovereign impunity" (Act V Scene 2).

Seducing and deceiving

Nevertheless, both Tartuffe and Dom Juan use this mask to seduce. Tartuffe abuses Orgon's and Mrs. Pernelle's credulity, who are ready to deny their own family for his benefit. Dom Juan calls upon Heaven to seduce Charlotte (Act II Scene 3), and plays his role so well that Dom Louis believes in his conversion, as does Sganarelle: "Ah! Sir, you are converted! You are converted! I have waited a very long time for this, and now, thanks to Heaven, all my wishes are fulfilled" (Act V Scene 2).

HYPOCRISY, A PRIVILEGED VICE

The part of the devotees

For the one as for the other, hypocrisy is a privileged vice. In Act V of *Dom Juan*, Molière settles his score with those who had *Tartuffe* banned and accused him of attacking true faith, when in truth he was only denouncing its parody, religious hypocrisy. There is a leap from Dom Juan's "I" to the impersonal form and the present tense of the general truths in sayings that describe the sins of the century: "Hypocrisy is a fashionable vice, and all fashionable vices pass for virtues" (Act V Scene 2).

The cloak of religion

At the time, nobody dared attack the devotees. Denouncing an impostor was risking to touch a man of true faith and to sully the sacred mysteries. Some people "have made for themselves a shield from the coat of religion, and [...] under this respectable garment, are still permitted to be the worst of men" (Act V Scene 2). Dom Juan will not part from his "sweet habits" and Tartuffe invites Elmire to give in to his advances (Act III Scene 3), using the devotees' impunity as an argument, explaining that it is a guarantee of secrecy: "Men of my sort, however, love discreetly/ and one may trust our reticence completely" (Act III Scene 3).

The power of the cabal

Thus, the hypocrites, knowing themselves to be guilty, are all accomplices ("What shocks one of their number, sends all to arms", Act VI Scene 2), and support each other, both through the law of silence, which guarantees their impunity, and through the violence of their attacks. In order not to be judged as what they truly are, they become the judges of others: "I will establish myself as a censor of others, judge badly of all, and have a good opinion of none but myself"

(Act V Scene 2).

THE ARREST OF THE IMPOSTOR AND THE DIVINE PUNISHMENT OF THE LIBERTINE

Molière condemns his characters

Although Dom Juan's libertinism can be appealing, he becomes odious, like Tartuffe, when he uses religion to abuse men. In *Tartuffe*, Molière takes the precaution of stating in one of his stage directions that "It is a scoundrel who talks" (Act IV, Scene 5), just as he writes in *Dom Juan* "playing the hypocrite" (Act V Scene 1). The entire art of the hypocrite being the wearing of a mask, Molière will finally unmask his characters to show their true face to the audience, the depths of their soul, to make sure that the audience will henceforth be impervious to their charms.

The final punishment

The two characters' dimension is measured according to their punishment. As a tribute to Louis XIV who supported Molière's play, Tartuffe is arrested as a crook by the king's emissary, "to whom all sham is hateful" (Act V Scene 7), who in this play has the role of the deus ex machina. As for Dom Juan, he will face death alone.

Dom Juan's death

It is God Himself who sends Dom Juan to hell, in a spectacular scene where the sun-like character, in a golden costume and flame-colored ribbons, is illuminated one last time by a blinding light: "Thunder resounds and great lightning-bolts surround Don Juan" (Act V Scene 6). It is a *pièce à machines* and as opposed to classical theatre, Dom Juan dies on stage. It is a way to convey to the audience the torment of damnation and to inspire "terror and pity", as in a tragedy: "O Heaven! What do I feel? An invisible fire burns me, I can move no more, and my whole body is turning to a glowing coal. Ah!" (Act V Scene 6). First burnt by the fire of love, in the end he dies in the fires of hell.

CHARACTERISTICS OF THE BAROQUE

The Baroque was born in Italy in the second half of the 16th century, as a consequence of the Counter-Reform (the catholic reform led in the 16th century against the protestant reform). The word, which comes from the Portuguese *barroco*, designates an irregularly carved gemstone, and was first used with a negative connotation to condemn an aestheticism that was breaking away from the classical ideal.

Movement and the distortion of forms

The adherents of the Baroque believe that everything is movement: man is a mortal creature, whose feelings are forever inconstant; time flees, nature is perpetually changing. Therefore, they reject the linear art of classicism, which evokes a stable world, in favor of the curve and the broken line, which suggest imbalance. Poetry describes the elusive movement of water, the consuming flame, the destroying power of time.

Masks and metamorphoses

This feeling of instability brought some adherents of the Baroque to consider the universe itself as nothing but a game of unclear reflections. Is life a dream? How can we distinguish between what is and what seems to be, between the face and the mask? In art, the trompe l'oeil, the décor, the façade, all concerned with appearance, grew more important. In the court theatre and ballet, disguise and adornments became well-loved.

Ostentation and excess

In an unstable world, the proud affirmation of the self is a way to rival with greatness (God, Nature), to fight against that which may enslave mankind (civil, moral or religious laws). Hyperbole, which involves the exaggeration of an idea, is thus the most favored figure of speech of the Baroque and the embodiment of this desire for overachievement.

The perception of death

Although some Baroque thinkers celebrate inconsistency as a way to free mankind – these thinkers being libertines as far as faith and morals are concerned, others, who are deeply religious, consider this frailty as a reminder of the misery of a man without God. Painters, in "vanities", show objects of human knowledge or worldly glory beside a skull, to remind us that we are: "memento mori" (Remember that you will die).

DOM JUAN, A BAROQUE CHARACTER?

Movement and distortion of forms

Dom Juan is a man of desire, and is therefore spontaneous and inconstant. To allow for this perpetual change of places and women - as both are linked - Molière rejects the rule of the unity of place and uses hyperbole to show a character who is too big for the limits of our world: "Like Alexander, I wish that there were other worlds, so I could march in and make my amorous conquests there as well" (Act I Scene 2).

Masks and metamorphoses

Dom Juan is a proteiform character, whose traits are no longer visible under his successive masks. In the scene with the beggar, he shows in turns the black face of the tempter, then the face of the knight in armor, as he comes to the aid of a man attacked by three ruffians. Moreover, in a world where hypocrisy, this "privileged vice" who takes the appearance of virtue, triumphs, one has to wear a mask "out of pure policy" and to "profit from the weakness of men" (Act V Scene 2).

Ostentation and excess

The magnificence of his golden costume, as described by Pierrot, shows Dom Juan's love for ostentatious adornments made to seduce and deceive. This excess is echoed in his desire for conquests that surpass the restricted limits of our world, and in his feeling of superiority as a great lord which places him above the human laws and brings him to challenge God: the character therefore has nearly superhuman dimensions, which has contributed to his myth.

The perception of death

Fear of death does not seem to affect Dom Juan ("nothing rattles me", Act IV Scene 7), nor does he fear the warnings of men or the signs from the Heavens. But Death casts its shadow over the whole play and the final punishment is announced from the first scene onwards. The death of the character is spectacularly staged as per Baroque fashion, both dark and flamboyant, constituting an oxymoron, an alliance of contraries.

THE MYTH OF DON JUAN

The origins

Don Juan was first mentioned in *The Trickster of Seville and the Stone Guest* (1630), an educative work by a monk, Tirso de Molina, in which a great lord defies the laws of God and men and dies in the fires of Hell. The play then arrived in Italy where it was changed into a farcical comedy, then in France, under the title *The Feast with the Statue*. In 1665, Molière took over the successful play.

What is a myth?

The expression of the deepest aspirations or conflicts of mankind, a character becomes a myth when he surpasses the framework of the work which created him. After Molière, who gave this complex character its full measure in a play where the supernatural also has a role to play, Dom Juan would later be used again and interpreted differently according to the period.

MOLIÈRE'S DOM JUAN

The great lord

The "great lord become an evil man" displays all the aristocratic qualities, but in an diverted way: seeking only pleasure in love, brave in duels, he despises men and scorns God out of natural habits of pride and courage, which are the result of his rank. While Tirso de Molina's character does not refrain from imploring God's mercy if it meant he could avoid damnation, Molière's Dom Juan refuses to see and hear the supernatural signs that are sent to him: "No, nothing strikes me with terror" (Act V Scene 5).

The final punishment

The punishment is equal to the challenge presented by Dom Juan to God and to men. If Molière uses him to condemn the atheist, the hypocrite and the great lord who has the audacity to place himself above the laws, in a time period attached to the rules of society, the place he gives him, the powers of seduction he attributes to him, are proof of a degree of hidden fascination.

EVOLUTION OF THE CHARACTER

In the 18th century, Lovelace in *Clarisse Harlowe* (written in 1748 by Samuel Richardson) and Valmont in *Dangerous Liaisons* (written by Choderlos de Laclos in 1782) inherited some of Dom Juan's traits: but from one century to the other, the "great lord become evil man" has become a scoundrel. Although the lightness of Mozart's music in the Italian opera *Don Giovanni* (1787) is an equivalent of the inconstancy of the libertine, Da Ponte, author of the libretto, condemns the character through the spectacular death of the finale, just as Molière did.

For the Romantics, Dom Juan is a hero of revolt, a man looking for the absolute. Musset, in his poem *Namouna* (1831) depicts him as looking for the unique woman through his numerous conquests. Baudelaire, in *Dom Juan in Hell* (1857), turns him into a proud figure of Satan.

The character was used again in the 20th century, to parody or sanctify it. The poet Milosz, in *Miguel Mañara* (1912), shows him touched by the grace of God's infinite love, the only love able to satisfy him. Conversely, Montherlant, in *La Mort qui fait le Trottoir* (1956), shows the age of the myth by showing a tired character of former beauty. The supernatural is suppressed.

FURTHER REFLECTION

SOME QUESTIONS TO THINK ABOUT…

- Explain the title: *Dom Juan or the Feast with the Statue*.
- Demonstrate to what extent the first scene of Act I is a scene of exposition.
- Explain Sganarelle's judgment of his master: "But a great lord become an evil man is a terrible thing" (Act I Scene 1)
- Can it be said that Sganarelle is Dom Juan's inferior double?
- What were the different meanings of the word 'libertine' in the 17th century? How does Dom Juan embody them all?
- In the portrait Dom Juan paints of himself to justify his inconstancy, he compares himself to Alexander the Great. Explain why.
- Molière's play does not follow the classical rule of the three unities (unity of place, time, and action). Explain why.
- To what extent is Molière's work a 'pièce à machines'?
- How important are spectacular stage effects in Molière's play?
- Why does Dom Juan pretend to be a devotee in Act V?
- How does Dom Juan belong to the Baroque aesthetic?
- Explain why the figure of Dom Juan has become a legend.

We want to hear from you!
Leave a comment on your online library
and share your favourite books on social media!

FURTHER READING

REFERENCE EDITION

- Molière (2006) *Dom Juan*. Paris: Éditions Larousse.

MORE FROM BRIGHTSUMMARIES.COM

- Reading guide - *The Miser* by Molière
- Reading guide – *The School for Wives* by Molière
- Reading guide – *Tartuffe* by Molière

Bright ≡Summaries.com

BOOK ANALYSIS

More guides to rediscover your love of literature

www.brightsummaries.com

©BrightSummaries.com, 2016. All rights reserved.

www.brightsummaries.com

Ebook EAN: 9782806270375

Paperback EAN: 9782806272843

Legal Deposit: D/2015/12603/579

Cover: © Primento

Digital conception by Primento, the digital partner of publishers.

Printed in Great Britain
by Amazon